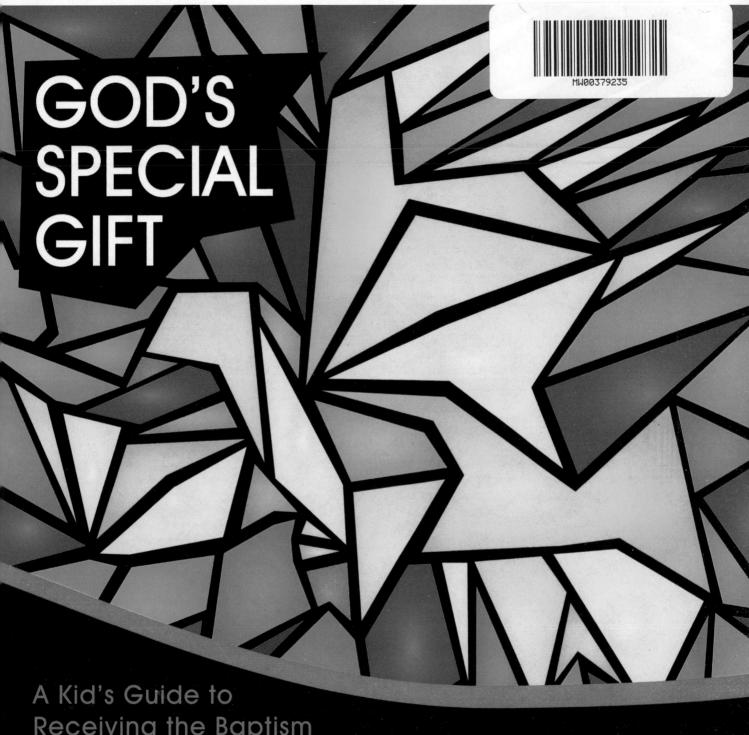

GOD'S SPECIAL GIFT

A Kid's Guide to
Receiving the Baptism
in the Holy Spirit

written & illustrated by Art Thomas

Endorsement:

"Art Thomas has produced a remarkable resource for those who desire to pass on the rich legacy of Pentecostal experience to their children. *God's Special Gift*, an invitation to experience the Pentecostal gift presented in narrative form, is theologically sound, artistically rich, and creatively captivating. This beautifully designed book will bless both parent and child as together they learn about and experience the richness of baptism in the Holy Spirit."

Robert Menzies
*Director of the Asian Center
for Pentecostal Theology*
www.Pentecost.asia

I dedicate this book to my two boys,
Josiah and Jeremiah Thomas.
May you grow into everything God
has planned for you to be.

Your dad believes in you. Go change the world.

SUPERNATURAL TRUTH PRODUCTIONS, LLC
Practical Training for Spirit-Filled Living
www.SupernaturalTruth.com

ISBN: 0692654070
ISBN-13: 978-0692654071

<u>Read This First...</u>

DEAR PARENTS,

Parenthood is a big deal. Jesus told us to make disciples of all nations, but the first disciples for whom we are responsible live within our own homes. As parents, we are the ones primarily responsible for the spiritual formation of our children, and that's why I wrote this book.

As an Assemblies of God minister and fellow parent of young children, I know how hard it is to find quality resources that help train our children with a Spirit-filled, Christian worldview. I wrote this book with the Pentecostal/Charismatic family in mind so that you can sensibly present the baptism in the Holy Spirit to your kids.

But this book is only one small part of the equation. You're still the leading spiritual coach in your child's life. Given that, I want to give you a few pointers that will help as you make disciples of the young ones you're raising.

First, make spirituality a normal part of your home life. Pray with your kids often. My boys are currently 3 and 5, and both already understand how to minister healing and do it regularly—not because I gave them a special teaching but because healing ministry is part of the culture of our home. Whatever you model in your home, you will reproduce. Since the topic at hand is the baptism in the Holy Spirit, be sure to model a Spirit-filled lifestyle. Let your kids see you praying for strangers, sharing the Gospel, loving people, operating in gifts of the Spirit, and even praying in tongues. Whatever they see, they will likely one day be.

Second, remember that the first priority is your child's salvation and relationship with God. If your child doesn't yet have a relationship with Jesus, you will want to share the Good News about Jesus with them before tackling the topic of this book. One of the first pages in this book summarizes the Gospel, but it is by no means a complete presentation. Make sure your children know the true stories about Jesus' life and ministry, His death and resurrection, and what it means to trust Him for salvation. Kids don't have to understand all the theological details. As long as there's a basic comprehension of the Gospel and a love for Jesus, they're ready for the content of this book.

Third, be aware that this book will likely raise more questions than it answers (kids are experts at asking questions even when we actually have explained something adequately!). You don't need to know all the answers, but you do need to model how to search out the answers. Teach them to look for things in the Bible. Bring them with you to ask your pastor or another Christian mentor in your life. Never be afraid to admit that you don't know something. Your children will respect you for it.

Fourth, be sure to read this book yourself before you read it to your child. Make sure you understand what is happening on each page. If you've never been baptized in the Holy Spirit yourself, you may find that this book helps lead you into your own encounter even as an adult. On the last page of this book, you'll find a list of page numbers and scripture references. So if you have any questions about anything in this book, find the corresponding page number and read the referenced scriptures for that page. You will likely find whatever you're looking for there.

Finally, if you pray for your child to be baptized in the Holy Spirit, make it a low-pressure experience. Don't try and force them. Pray for them, and lay your hands on them. Sometimes pray together; other times, let them seek this Gift alone. The emphasis is power for the mission, so help them to think about people who need to know Jesus. This will help them realize that they're asking God to help them minister to others. If it's taking a while, encourage them that this is normal and that some kids take a longer time to experience God in this way. Encourage them to continue seeking God for power until they have the evidence of speaking in tongues. It won't be long before they are baptized in the Holy Spirit and discover the synergy of partnering with Him to speak in tongues. And when that happens, rejoice with them! Encourage them to pray in that new prayer language often and especially to engage in the mission Jesus gave us.

I pray God richly blesses you and your family through this book and the discussions and prayers that it ignites.

Art Thomas

Art Thomas, Author

Hi! I'm Andrew, and I want to tell you about one of the most amazing things that ever happened to me.

I'm what some people would call a disciple, which means I follow and learn from Jesus. Sometimes people call me an apostle, which means Jesus sent me to help lead His people in loving the world and teaching others about Him.

But I just like to think of myself as Jesus' friend because that's the word He used. Not only that, but Jesus has a special Gift for all His friends, and that's what I want to tell you about today.

2

You've probably heard about how Jesus died on a cross and then came back to life. That one powerful act changed me forever.

Even though I had done many things in my life that made God sad, Jesus experienced the pain and death that I deserved. He forgave me and made me a different person who no longer does the bad things I used to do!

The same Holy Spirit who raised Jesus from the dead now lives inside of me. I'm a completely new person, and I finally understand what it's like to be truly alive!

Anyone who trusts Jesus to change their life can have the same experience. Even you!

But there's MORE! There's that special Gift. God gave this Gift to me, and He wants to give it to you too!

After Jesus died and rose again, He made a wonderful promise to me and all His other friends. He said that when the Holy Spirit comes on us, we would receive power.

The same way John the Baptist used to baptize people in the Jordan River, Jesus promised to baptize us in the Holy Spirit—and that's how we receive His special Gift. Instead of being dipped in water and being covered in water, He promised to cover us with power from His Holy Spirit.

Do you know what that means?

Long before Jesus came to earth, the Holy Spirit came upon many people and gave them power to do amazing things for God.

He came upon Moses and the elders of Israel to help them lead God's people.

He came upon a man named Sampson to give him super-powered strength.

He came upon prophets...

...priests...

...and kings.

And the most common thing people did when the Holy Spirit came upon them is prophesy, which means that God began to speak through them to others.

But this sort of thing was rare. It only happened to really special people who God wanted to empower for a very special purpose.

Nevertheless, God spoke through a man named Joel and promised something amazing. God said that one day, He would pour out His Holy Spirit on everyone!

It doesn't matter if you are young or old.

It doesn't matter if you are a boy or a girl.

It doesn't matter if you are rich or poor.

God promised that everyone who serves Him would one day receive power from the Holy Spirit so that all His people could prophesy and do all sorts of amazing things for Him.

One time, John the Baptist baptized Jesus in the Jordan River. When Jesus came up out of the water, God's Holy Spirit came upon Him gently, like a dove. John said that this was a sign proving that Jesus would baptize people in the Holy Spirit, covering them with God's power.

11

From that moment forward, Jesus began to show us some things we can do after He baptizes us in the Holy Spirit—and He did some pretty amazing things!

He healed people.

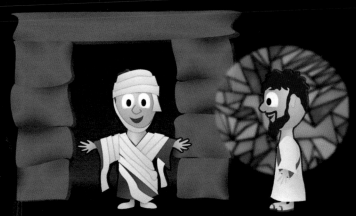

He brought some dead people back to life.

He did amazing miracles.

He prophesied and did many good and kind things.

If Father God wanted Jesus to do something, Jesus could do it. The Holy Spirit gives us power to help us obey God— even if God wants us to do something impossible!

After Jesus died and rose again, Father God took Jesus up into heaven. But before Jesus left, He told my friends and me to tell everyone everywhere the good news about Him. He also said that He wanted us to have the same power He had so that we could say and do the same amazing things that He said and did.

Even though He wanted us to go all over the world with His good news, He told us to first wait where we were until the same Holy Spirit who had already changed our hearts also came upon us to give us power.

So we waited for God to fulfill His promise. And do you know what happened next?

A few days later was a big feast day called Pentecost. We were all together in someone's house when we heard a big sound like a powerful wind. Something that looked like fire swirled above us. The fire split apart, and then the different parts came down to rest on each of us.

We knew it meant that God had given us power to prophesy; but when we started to talk, we found ourselves speaking languages we didn't even understand!

All our noise drew a crowd. Some of the people in the crowd came from places where they knew the languages we were speaking. And even though we didn't know what we were saying, they said we were speaking wonderful things about God!

We went outside, and my friend Peter told them that what they saw wasn't crazy. He told them about God's promise through Joel and said that God had poured out His Spirit upon us. Then he told them all about Jesus. Three thousand people decided to follow Jesus that day!

After that, we went everywhere, telling people about how good God is and everything Jesus did. We told them that God wanted to forgive them and change their lives, just like He had changed ours.

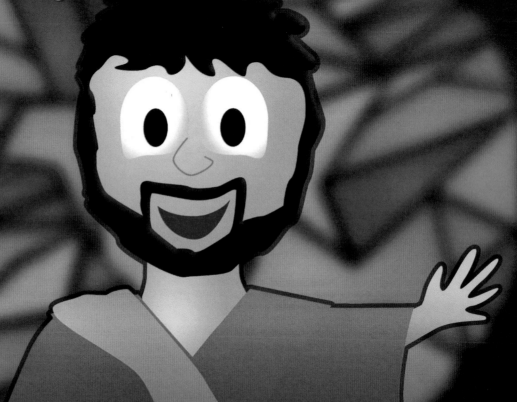

Everywhere we went, God's Holy Spirit helped us to prophesy, teach, love, help, give, and more. Even when people didn't like our good news, we told them about God's love for them and refused to give up.

Many people were healed, some were raised from the dead, powerful miracles happened, and many more people decided to believe in Jesus and follow Him like we do.

My friend Philip told people about Jesus in a different place called Samaria. Many miracles happened there, and the people of that town were filled with joy.

When they found out about what happened, my friends Peter and John traveled there to pray for all the new believers to receive power from the Holy Spirit, and they all did. Now the new believers in Samaria could do the works of Jesus too!

God's good news was spreading to new people, just like

Later, my friend Peter went to share the good news about Jesus with a group of people from a different country. They were all gathered at the home of a man named Cornelius.

Even before Peter was done telling them about Jesus, they all began prophesying and speaking other languages just like we did when the Holy Spirit came upon us!

Whenever the Holy Spirit helps people speak languages they don't understand, we call this "speaking in tongues." And when Peter heard the people speaking in tongues, he knew God had given them power to help them spread God's good news to new people.

Another time, in a far-away city called Ephesus, another of Jesus' friends—named Paul—found some people who believed in God but had never had the Holy Spirit come upon them.

When Paul placed his hands on each of them, they began speaking in tongues and praising God too!

It doesn't matter where you live or how long you've been following Jesus. God loves to give power to everyone who follows Jesus so that we can all show His love and tell other people the good news about Him.

God has promised to pour His Holy Spirit on everyone who believes in Jesus—including you! He does this so that you can have power to show His love to people who have never heard about Him.

His power can give you just the right words to say that will help someone believe in Jesus.

And the Holy Spirit will make you bold too! That means you won't be afraid to tell anybody about Jesus.

If you love Jesus and have chosen to trust Him to change your life like I have, and if you want to obey Him by telling people about Him like I do, then you can receive God's power just like me!

As a follower of Jesus, God's Holy Spirit already lives inside of you. He's there to give you love, joy, peace, patience, kindness, goodness, faithfulness, gentleness, and self-control. He can speak to your heart, encourage you to do the right thing, and help you grow into the person God intends for you to be.

But if you ask Jesus to baptize you in the Holy Spirit, then that same Holy Spirit will overflow and cover you with power on the outside too.

Then you too will be able to prophesy, speak in tongues, and do any other powerful thing that God wants you to do with His help!

I don't know what your experience will feel like. It's different for everyone.

When God's Holy Spirit came upon Jesus, He came like a dove.

When He came upon my friends and me, He came like fire.

When He came upon the people in Samaria and Ephesus, He came in a different way as my friends prayed for them.

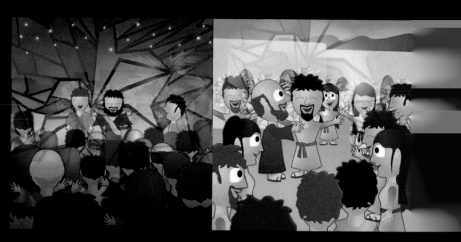

And when He came upon those people from another country, there was no dove, no fire, and no one praying for them. Peter simply told them about Jesus!

Your experience doesn't have to be like anyone else's. The only thing that matters is that the same Holy Spirit who lives inside of you covers you with His power. And remember, Jesus is the One who makes it all possible. Even though you can't see Him, He will baptize you in the Holy Spirit just like He baptized me

All you have to do is rest. Ask Jesus to baptize you in the Holy Spirit. Then simply wait quietly until you realize the Holy Spirit is covering you with power.

You might feel something or you might not. You might have deep peace in your heart or become very excited. Again, it doesn't matter what it's like. Just know that it's the Holy Spirit and that Jesus is answering your prayer.

No matter what the Holy Spirit does when He comes upon you—no matter what your experience feels like—when it happens, you will be able to speak in tongues just like my friends and I did. You won't know what you're saying, but you'll know it's not coming from your own imagination.

And it's really easy too! All you have to do is start speaking whatever sounds you feel deep inside of you, and the Holy Spirit will help you to speak a beautiful language just like He helped my friends and me.

God loves to give His Holy Spirit to everyone who asks Him. Don't give up if nothing happens the first time you ask. Take time with God, and let Him help you to experience His Holy Spirit.

The language God gives you is a gift, and whenever we pray to God with our new language, we are encouraged and strengthened. Even though you don't understand what you're saying, God does, and your friendship with Him will grow deeper and stronger.

34

And that's it!

When you have received this amazing gift from God, you have the same power Jesus had—power to obey the Father and do whatever amazing things He wants you to do.

You can see people healed when you put your hands on them.

You can see miracles happen when you obey God.

You can prophesy when God speaks to your heart and tells you a message for someone else.

And most importantly, you can show people God's love and tell them the good news about what Jesus has done for them.

The Holy Spirit loves to tell people about Jesus; so whenever you tell people about Jesus, the Holy Spirit loves to help!

Jesus wants everyone to know Him, and that's why He baptizes His friends in the Holy Spirit. He wants to help you share His good news and love with everyone.

Scripture References

The following list of Scripture references will help bring clarity to some of the concepts presented in this book. Some passages refer to the scene depicted in a particular illustration while others pertain to one specific phrase within the written content. Still others apply to the overarching concept on the page. Since space is limited, I couldn't include every single reference pertaining to each topic, but this should at least help point you in the right direction.

1   Jn. 15:15
2   Mk. 3:13-18
3   Mt. 26-28; Rom. 6:23; 2 Cor. 5:16-21
4   Rom. 8:11; Eph. 2:1-10
5   Lk. 24:49; Acts 1:8
6   Jn. 1:35-40; Acts 1:1-5
7   Num. 11:25-26; Jdg. 14:5-6
8   1 Sam. 16:13; 19:18-24; 2 Kng. 2:15; 2 Chron. 24:20; Ez. 11:5
9   Joel 2:28-29; Acts 2:17-18
10   Joel 2:28-29; Acts 2:17-18
11   Mt. 3:16; Mk. 1:10; Lk. 3:21-22; Jn. 1:32-33
12   Four Gospels; Jn. 5:19; 14:12; 21:25
13   Mt. 28:16-20; Mk. 16:15-20; Lk. 24:45-53; Jn. 20:21; Acts 1:1-11
14   Acts 1:1-11
15   Acts 2:1-4
16   Acts 2:5-41
17   Mk. 16:20; Acts 3-4; 8:1-4
18   Book of Acts (Illustration: Acts 3:1-8)

19   Acts 8:5-8
20   Acts 8:14-17
21   Acts 10
22   Acts 10:27,44
23   Acts 19:1-7
24   Acts 19:6
25   Lk. 12:11-12; Acts 2:38-39; 4:31
26   Acts 2:38-39
27   Jn. 16:12-15; Rom. 15:16; 8:13; Gal. 5:16-17; 5:22-23; 2 Thes. 2:13; 2 Tim. 1:7; 1 Pet. 1:2
28   Lk. 24:49; Jn. 7:37-39; 14:12;
29   Mt. 3:16; Acts 2:3
30   Acts 8:15,17; 10:44; 19:6
31   1 Cor. 14:14
32   Acts 2:4; 1 Cor. 14:14
33   Lk. 11:11-13; 1 Cor. 14:2,4,18
35   Mk. 16:17-18; Jn. 14:12; Acts 2:17-18; 1 Cor. 14:31
36   Mk. 16:15; Jn. 15:26; Rev. 19:10

Red text indicates the page number while blue text is the Scripture reference.